America's
ANIMAL
COMEBACKS

Gray Wolves
Return to Yellowstone

by Meish Goldish

Consultant: Douglas W. Smith, Ph.D.
Yellowstone Wolf Project Leader

BEARPORT
PUBLISHING

New York, New York

Credits

Cover and Title Page © Christophe Namur/istockphoto.com; 4–5, © Yellowstone National Park Service; 5, © Yellowstone National Park Service; 6, © Tom Brakefield/CORBIS; 7, © Images.com/Nostalgia/Stock Illustration Source/Getty Images; 8, © Layne Kennedy/CORBIS; 9, © The Denver Public Library, Western History Collection, Call Number 11001557; 10, © Monty Sloan/www.Wolfphotography.com; 11, © Aldo Leopold Foundation; 13, © Robert Nunnington/The Image Bank/Gallo Images/Getty Images; 14, © Yellowstone National Park Service; 15L, © Yellowstone National Park Service; 15R, © Yellowstone National Park Service; 16–17, © Yellowstone National Park Service; 18, © Yellowstone National Park Service; 19, © Barry O'Neil/National Park Service/Time Life Pictures/Getty Images; 20, © Yellowstone National Park Service; 21, © Yellowstone National Park Service; 21 Inset, © Yellowstone National Park Service; 22, © JessLeePhotos.com; 23, © John Eastcott and Yva Momatiuk/National Geographic/Getty Images; 25, © Monte Dolack; 26, © Yellowstone National Park Service; 27, © Jeff Vanuga/CORBIS; 28, © DLILLC/Corbis; 29T, © Millard H. Sharp/Photo Researchers, Inc.; 29B, © PHONE Cordier Sylvain/Peter Arnold, Inc.; 31, © AJE/Shutterstock and © Robert J. Beyers II/Shutterstock.

Publisher: Kenn Goin
Editorial Director: Adam Siegel
Creative Director: Spencer Brinker
Photo Researcher: Beaura Kathy Ringrose
Cover Design: Dawn Beard Creative

Library of Congress Cataloging-in-Publication Data

Goldish, Meish.
  Gray wolves : return to Yellowstone / by Meish Goldish.
      p. cm. — (America's animal comebacks)
  Includes bibliographical references and index.
  ISBN-13: 978-1-59716-502-0 (library binding)
  ISBN-10: 1-59716-502-6 (library binding)
  1. Wolves—Reintroduction—Yellowstone National Park. I. Title.

  QL737.C22G59 2007
  599.77309787'52—dc22

                          2007005108

For more information, write to Bearport Publishing Company, Inc., 101 Fifth Avenue, Suite 6R, New York, New York, 10003. Printed in the United States of America.

10 9 8 7 6 5 4 3 2

Contents

A Bold Plan

The scientists at Yellowstone **National Park** watched the gray wolves with hope and excitement. These wild animals had been brought to the park from Alberta, Canada, as part of a **bold** plan.

In 1995, there were no wolves in all of Yellowstone. There hadn't been any for nearly 70 years. Would the 14 wolves from Canada have **pups** and **repopulate** the park?

The wolves were kept in pens before being released into the park.

No one knew if the plan would work. At best, the animals would live in Yellowstone as they once had for thousands of years. At worst, they would be killed, like so many wolves before them.

Children got the day off from school to see the wolves return to Yellowstone National Park.

The last wolf in Yellowstone was killed in 1926.

Once Upon a Time

Life for wolves hadn't always been so bad. About 400 years ago, two million wolves roamed freely in North America. There was land for them to live on. There was food for them to eat. The **Native Americans** who lived near the wolves respected the animals for their hunting skills.

In the 1600s, however, people from Europe began **settling** in America. They felt the creatures were harmful and dangerous. Popular fairy tales told of the "big bad wolf" that attacked people. Farmers hated the animals because they killed their **livestock**, such as sheep and cattle. As a result, people began to kill wolves. Hunters were paid a **bounty** for every wolf they killed.

Wolves hunt animals for food. However, they avoid people as much as possible and almost never attack them.

In many popular children's stories, wolves are shown to be dangerous to people.

From Bad to Worse

In the 1800s, life for wolves in North America grew much worse. **Pioneers** moved across the American West. They built farms and ranches on land where wolves lived. They also killed animals, such as bison, that wolves hunted for food. With fewer bison to eat, the wolves began killing the ranchers' cows. So hunters set out traps and poison for the animals. The wolves, once known as hunters, were now the hunted.

Settlers used steel traps like this one to catch wolves.

Every year, thousands of wolves were killed. By the early 1900s, nearly all the wolves in North America were gone. Scientists wondered if the **endangered** creatures would soon become **extinct**.

Wolves killed by hunters in the mid-1900s

Between 1850 and 1900, as many as one million wolves may have been killed in the United States.

A New Way of Thinking

In the 1930s, people began to think differently about wolves. Scientists learned that the animals kill **prey**, such as elk and deer, that are old and sick. Hunting these weaker animals means that the healthier ones are left to **breed** and find food. So wolves actually help other groups of animals stay strong.

Scientists who studied wolves stopped seeing them as harmful **predators**. Instead, they saw them as an important part of nature's **ecosystem**. They wanted to try to bring wolves back to places in North America where they had disappeared. Yellowstone National Park seemed the perfect place to start. Its ecosystem was complete except for one thing—wolves.

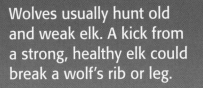

Wolves usually hunt old and weak elk. A kick from a strong, healthy elk could break a wolf's rib or leg.

In 1944, Aldo Leopold was the first scientist to suggest bringing wolves back to Yellowstone. It would take more than 50 years for his idea to become a reality.

Aldo Leopold

Welcome to Yellowstone

Scientists were excited to bring wolves back to Yellowstone. It is one of the most popular national parks in the world. It is known for its beautiful mountains, forests, and lakes. Yellowstone is also famous for its **wildlife**. Bears, elk, beavers, bison, and bald eagles live there.

Montana

Idaho

Wyoming

Yellowstone National Park

C A N A D A

U N I T E D

S T A T E S

Pacific Ocean

M E X I C O

Atlantic Ocean

N
W   E
S

☐ Yellowstone National Park

Yellowstone National Park covers more than two million acres (809,371 hectares) of land. It stretches into parts of three states—Wyoming, Idaho, and Montana.

Most important, Yellowstone is a safe place for its animals. Hunting is against the law there, as it is in any national park. It is also against the law to cut down trees or harm any plants.

Yellowstone National Park was named the world's first national park in 1872.

Making a Plan

The program to bring wolves back to Yellowstone was called the Yellowstone Wolf Project. Two of its leaders were Mike Phillips and Doug Smith. The program took a great deal of planning.

First, **biologists** had to capture wolves in Canada. To do this, they needed to fly in helicopters and shoot the animals with darts to make them fall asleep. The wolves could then be safely put in crates and brought to the park.

Each wolf was brought to Yellowstone in a crate.

Next, Mike and Doug needed a way to keep track of the animals in the park. They decided to use special collars that would be placed around each wolf's neck. The collars would send out radio signals to let scientists track the animals' movements.

A wolf radio collar

Doug Smith places a radio collar around a wolf's neck.

Wolves live in a group, or **pack**, of around ten family members. The 14 wolves from Canada were placed into three packs—the Crystal Creek pack, the Rose Creek pack, and the Soda Butte pack.

Life in a Pen

Once the wolves were brought to Yellowstone, Mike and Doug had to decide how to release them into the park. A *hard release* would mean simply letting the wolves immediately run free in the park. The scientists, however, chose a *soft release*. They kept the wolves in a large, fenced-in area called an **acclimation pen**. Each wolf pack stayed in its own pen for about ten weeks before it was set free.

There were good reasons for keeping each pack in a pen. Mike and Doug hoped that the wolves would **bond** with one another during their ten-week period together. They did not want the pack to split up after leaving the pen. They also hoped the wolves would not try to return to Canada once they were set loose.

Each acclimation pen at Yellowstone is nearly one acre (.4 hectare) in size. Armed guards protected the pens 24 hours a day.

A wolf being released from a crate into an acclimation pen

Leaders of the Pack

One pen held the Rose Creek pack. Two of its wolves were called 9F and 10M. 9F was a female. 10M was a male. Each was an **alpha wolf**, or leader of the pack.

Alpha is the first letter of the Greek alphabet. An alpha wolf is one of the two top-ranked wolves in a pack.

Female wolf 9F

Alpha wolves decide where the pack will travel and sleep. They are usually the only wolves in a pack to breed. Mike and Doug hoped that 9F and 10M would produce pups. However, they were not sure if the two alpha wolves would even like each other. Only time would tell. In March 1995, the wolves were set loose in Yellowstone.

Male wolf 10M

Keeping Track

Mike and Doug used the radio collars to track the wolves' movements in the park. To their relief, 9F and 10M stayed together. However, they soon left Yellowstone. The two alpha wolves settled near a small Montana town just outside the park.

Scientists in a plane can track the signal from a wolf's radio collar that is 10 to 30 miles (16 to 48 km) away.

On April 24, 1995, a hunter spotted and killed 10M. He tried to hide the body. However, the wolf's radio collar led police to the hunter, who was **fined** $10,000 and jailed.

Mike and Doug feared that 10M had left no pups behind. Luckily, they were wrong. On May 3, 1995, eight wolf pups produced by 9F and 10M were discovered.

9F and 10M's pups were rescued and brought back to Yellowstone.

A female wolf usually gives birth to 5 or 6 pups at a time, but she may have up to 11.

Changes in the Park

Most of the gray wolves introduced in 1995 **adapted** to Yellowstone and survived. The next year, 17 more wolves were released into the park.

Soon, the park began to change for the better. Plants and animals were growing healthier and stronger. The wolves had improved Yellowstone's ecosystem. How did it happen?

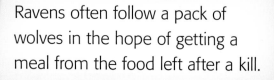

Ravens often follow a pack of wolves in the hope of getting a meal from the food left after a kill.

The Yellowstone wolves provided more food for other animals in the park. After the wolves killed and fed on an elk, the leftovers were eaten by ravens, eagles, and coyotes.

By hunting sick and old elk, wolves cut down the number of animals that ate plants and trees. Soon there were more homes for birds. There was more plant food for beavers. The number of birds and beavers in Yellowstone increased, thanks to the wolves.

After a wolf pack kills a moose or an elk, it may soon be stolen by a grizzly bear for its own meal.

Success

Mike and Doug saw how the wolves had improved Yellowstone. The alpha wolves they had brought to the park had pups. Those pups grew up and started new packs. The plan seemed to be working.

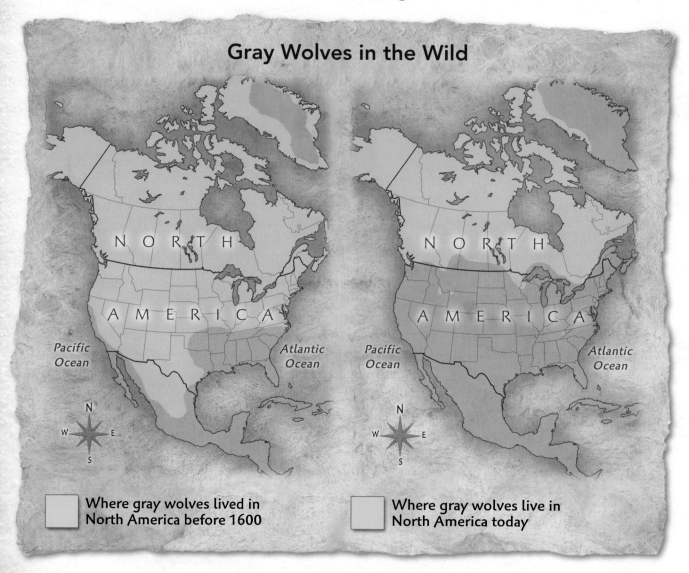

Gray Wolves in the Wild

☐ Where gray wolves lived in North America before 1600

☐ Where gray wolves live in North America today

These maps show where gray wolves have lived in North America in the past and where they live in the present.

Not everyone was happy, however. Many farmers worried that the new wolves would kill their livestock. The organization Defenders of Wildlife, however, had a plan to help them. They would pay farmers and ranchers for each animal they lost due to wolves.

This poster was created and sold to help raise money to pay farmers for animals killed by wolves.

If a Yellowstone wolf hunts and kills livestock outside of the park, ranchers are allowed to kill the animal.

The Future

The Yellowstone Wolf Project continues today. It is considered a great success. Scientists are pleased with the growing number of gray wolves in Yellowstone. After just over 10 years, about 136 wolves now roam through the park. There are around 13 wolf packs.

Tourists come from around the world to watch the wolves at Yellowstone.

The best times to see Yellowstone wolves are between sunrise and 8:00 A.M., and in the evening after 6:00 P.M. These are the times when wolves are most active.

"Wolves were the only mammal missing from Yellowstone," explained Doug Smith. "Now that they're back, the whole ecosystem is really back together. The return of the wolf is one of the best things to happen to Yellowstone in the past **century**."

Gray Wolf Facts

In 1973, Congress passed the Endangered **Species** Act. This law protects animals and plants that are in danger of dying out in the United States. Harmful activities, such as hunting, capturing, or collecting endangered species, are illegal under this act.

The gray wolf was one of the first species listed under the Endangered Species Act. Here are some other facts about the gray wolf.

Population: North American population in 1600: **2,000,000**
North American population today: **65,000**
World population today: about **150,000**

Height
2.5 feet (76 cm) tall at the shoulder

Length
5–6.5 feet (1.5–2 m) long, including the tail

Weight
75–120 pounds (34–54 kg)

Fur Color
gray, brown, white, or black

Food
moose, elk, deer, beavers, caribou, bison, musk ox, and rabbits

Life Span
about 2–5 years in the wild; about 8–10 years in captivity

Habitat
mainly Alaska, Canada, Minnesota, Mongolia, and Russia

Other Wolves in Danger

The gray wolves at Yellowstone are one kind of wolf that's making a comeback by increasing its numbers. Other types of wolves are also trying to make a comeback.

Red Wolf

- There are fewer than 300 red wolves in the world.
- Only about 100 live in the wild.
- Red wolves were once found in the southeastern United States, from Texas to Florida, and north to the Carolinas, Kentucky, Illinois, and Missouri.
- Today, red wolves have been reintroduced to the wild in North Carolina.

Ethiopian Wolf

- There are fewer than 550 Ethiopian wolves in the world.
- These animals are sometimes called Abyssinian wolves.
- They live in a country in northeastern Africa called Ethiopia.
- It is illegal to hunt Ethiopian wolves.
- Half of the Ethiopian wolf population lives in Bale Mountain National Park in southern Ethiopia.

Glossary

acclimation pen (*ak*-luh-MAY-shun PEN) a fenced-in area where animals are kept to give them time to get used to a new surrounding

adapted (uh-DAPT-id) changed in order to get along in a new surrounding

alpha wolf (AL-fuh WULF) one of the two highest-ranked wolves, a male and a female, in the pack

biologists (bye-OL-uh-jists) scientists who study plants or animals

bold (BOHLD) daring

bond (BOND) to form a close relationship

bounty (BOUN-tee) a reward offered for the capture of a harmful animal or person

breed (BREED) to produce young

century (SEN-chuh-ree) one hundred years

ecosystem (EE-koh-*siss*-tuhm) a community of animals and plants that depend on one another to live

endangered (en-DAYN-jurd) being in danger of dying out

extinct (ek-STINGKT) when a kind of plant or animal has died out; no more of its kind is living anywhere in the world

fined (FINED) ordered to pay an amount of money for doing something wrong

livestock (LIVE-*stok*) animals, such as sheep, chicken, or cows, that are raised on a farm or ranch

national park (NASH-uh-nuhl PARK) an area of land set aside by the government to protect the animals and plants that live there

Native Americans (NAY-tiv uh-MER-uh-kinz) the first people to live in America; they are sometimes called American Indians

pack (PAK) a group of wolves that live together

pioneers (*pye*-uh-NEERZ) the first people to live in a new area

predators (PRED-uh-turz) animals that hunt other animals for food

prey (PRAY) animals that are hunted or caught for food

pups (PUPS) baby wolves; short for "puppies"

repopulate (ree-POP-yuh-layt) to supply again with animals or people

settling (SET-uhl-ing) living or making a home in a new place

species (SPEE-sheez) groups that animals are divided into, according to similar characteristics; members of the same species can have offspring together

wildlife (WILDE-*life*) wild animals that are living in their natural environment

Bibliography

Bailey, Jill. *Gray Wolf (Animals Under Threat).* Chicago: Heinemann Library (2005).

Chadwick, Douglas H. "Return of the Gray Wolf," *National Geographic,* 193:5 (May 1998), pp. 77–99.

Smith, Douglas W., and Gary Ferguson. *Decade of the Wolf: Returning the Wild to Yellowstone.* Guilford, CT: The Lyons Press (2005).

Swinburne, Stephen R. *Once a Wolf: How Wildlife Biologists Fought to Bring Back the Gray Wolf.* Boston: Houghton Mifflin (1999).

Read More

Havard, Christian. *The Wolf: Night Howler.* Watertown, MA: Charlesbridge Publishing (2006).

Kalman, Bobbie. *Endangered Wolves.* New York: Crabtree Publishing (2005).

Parker, Barbara K. *North American Wolves.* Minneapolis, MN: Carolrhoda Books (1998).

Reiter, Chris. *The Gray Wolf (Endangered and Threatened Animals).* Berkeley Heights, NJ: Enslow Publishers (2003).

Learn More Online

To learn more about wolves and their return to Yellowstone, visit
www.bearportpublishing.com/AnimalComebacks

Index

About the Author

Meish Goldish has written more than 100 books for children. His book *Fossil Tales* won the Learning Magazine Teachers' Choice Award.